A GIFT

— FROM —

Mrs BEETON

EDIBLE DELIGHTS

A GIFT

— FROM —

Mrs BEETON

EDIBLE DELIGHTS

WARD LOCK

First published 1991 by Ward Lock
Villiers House, 41/47 Strand, London WC2N 5JE, England

A Cassell imprint

British Library Cataloguing in Publication Data
A gift from Mrs Beeton.
1. Food, History
641.300941

ISBN 0-7063-7038-4

Designed by Cherry Randell
Illustrations by Mike Shoebridge

Typeset in Goudy Old Style by Litho Link Ltd, Welshpool, Powys, Wales

Printed and bound in Italy

1 cup butter = 225 g/8 oz
1 cup caster (superfine) sugar = 200 g/7 oz
1 cup dried fruit = 150 g/5 oz
1 cup flour = 100 g/4 oz
1 cup honey = 350 g/12 oz
1 cup icing (confectioner's) sugar = 150 g/5 oz
1 cup loaf sugar = 175 g/6 oz
1 cup walnuts (chopped) = 100 g/4oz

◈◈◈◈◈◈◈◈◈◈◈◈◈◈◈◈◈◈

ONTENTS

$\mathscr{I}$NTRODUCTION

In today's world of freezers, canned goods and dehydrated foods, it is easy to forget how much more complicated it was for Victorian cooks to preserve food in times of plenty so that there was still a good supply during the harsh winter months. Fruit was either bottled in syrup, packed in jars with layers of sugar, crystallized or made into jams, jellies or pastes that were prepared by boiling the fruit pulp by itself and then with sugar. The mixture was then poured into a mould or tray and dried out in the oven.

As soon as fruit was ripe, it was brought into the kitchen and scullery maids and cooks had to drop almost every other task in order to prepare the fruit for the preserving pan before it started to spoil. In wealthy households jam was often made on a special

portable stove and trivet (to hold the pan well above the gas burners whose direct heat could cause the jam to stick) set up in a scullery away from the heat of the kitchen range.

Sugar was bought in large cones and had to be broken up before use. Egg-sized pieces were snapped or chipped off the block with a special chopper and iron nippers, and then carefully weighed. Watery fruits were boiled first to evaporate some of the liquid before the sugar was added, otherwise the jam would not set.

Vegetables were preserved in chutneys, pickles and other condiments, or they were salted. Chutneys were made with almost any leftover vegetables and fruit. Capers, cauliflowers, onions, walnuts, gherkins, cucumbers and mushrooms were pickled in vinegars. Ketchups (also called catsups) were made by steeping mushrooms, anchovies, walnuts or tomatoes in salt and then boiling the vegetables with spices and vinegar before straining them into bottles.

Careful sealing of pots and jars was vital if the pickles and preserves were to withstand the

damp of the store-room and the forays of rats and mice. Paper covers were fixed in place with egg white, or they were dipped in vinegar, brandy, melted wax or a hot flour and water paste before being tied on to the jar. Jars of preserved fruits were sometimes plugged with cork and resin or wax.

The making of jams and pickles demands as much care today as in Victorian times, although modern cookers, highly refined sugar, efficient storage jars and dry store cupboards assure a higher success rate. It is certainly worth the effort required, and handmade preserves and sweetmeats are a valuable addition to the family larder, and give enormous pleasure when offered as a gift.

JAMS AND JELLIES

As well as using surplus fresh fruit, home-made jams are much more delicious than commercially produced preserves which often contain unwanted additives. For perfect results, accurate weighing and measuring are essential.

PEACH OR APRICOT JAM

450 g/1 lb dried peaches **or** *apricots*
1.1 litres/2 pints water for peaches **or**
1.75 litres/3 pints for apricots
1.4 kg/3 lb loaf sugar
juice of 1 lemon
50–75 g/2–3 oz blanched almonds,
finely shredded (optional)

Wash the fruit and put in a bowl with the water. Soak for 24–48 hours.

Transfer the fruit and water to a preserving pan and simmer for 30 minutes, stirring occasionally. Add the sugar, lemon juice and shredded almonds. Stir over a low heat until the sugar is dissolved. Bring to the boil and boil rapidly until setting point is reached.

Skim. Pour into hot, dry jars and cover.

MAKES ABOUT 2.25 kg/5 lb

GREEN FIG JAM

300 ml/½ pint water
675 g/1½ lb loaf sugar
juice of 1 lemon
900 g/2 lb green figs

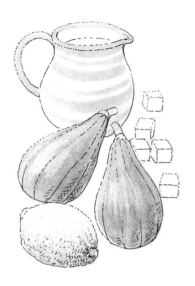

Put the water, sugar and lemon
juice in a saucepan, bring to the
boil and boil for 10 minutes.
Meanwhile cut the figs in slices.
Add the fruit to the syrup and boil
gently for about 1 hour, until
setting point is reached.

Skim. Pour into hot, dry jars and
cover.

MAKES ABOUT
1.4 kg/3 lb

◇◇

ESSENTIAL EQUIPMENT

Pan
A stainless steel pan is best. If using
a copper or brass pan, make sure
that any polish is carefully washed
off. Do not use chipped enamel,
iron or zinc.

Thermometers
An accurate thermometer, marked
up to or above 104°C/220°F, is
useful for testing the jam for setting
point.

Spoons
Wooden spoons are needed for
stirring, and a metal draining
spoon is useful for lifting off any
scum.

Pots and Jars
Use glass or stoneware pots which
must be clean, dry, and warm
before filling with the hot jam or
jelly.

CHOOSING FRUIT

Select fruit that is firm and ripe, or slightly underripe. (Greengages and gooseberries must be underripe.) This will have a full flavour and will keep well until it reaches the preserving pan. Overripe fruit will have lost its best flavour and will not set as jam. Store the fruit in a cool dry place or in a refrigerator.

Fruits varies considerably in the amount of sugar, acid and pectin it contains and can be divided into three groups:

Fruit which sets easily: apples, blackcurrants, damsons, gooseberries, plums and redcurrants.

Fruit of medium setting quality: apricots, blackberries, loganberries and raspberries.

Fruit which does not set easily and needs added pectin and acid: cherries and strawberries.

The amounts of added sugar, acid such as lemon juice, and pectin needed in each recipe depend on the natural content of each fruit.

The most suitable fruits for jelly-making are apples, bilberries, blackberries, crab apples, currants, damsons and quinces.

Discard any blemished fruit. Wash berries and wipe larger fruits carefully. Remove the stones from cherries, greengages and all plums before using; crack, blanch and skin a few kernels and add to the jam just before it is ready.

QUINCE PASTE

1.8 kg/4 lb quinces
1.8 kg/4 lb loaf sugar

Put the quinces into a saucepan with sufficient water to cover. Simmer until the fruit is soft, then mash and push through a sieve into a preserving pan.

Dissolve the sugar in 1.1 litres/2 pints water, bring to boiling point and skim. Boil the syrup to the 'small crack' degree (144°C/290°F), and pour over the fruit.

Put the pan over the heat, and stir the mixture well while boiling, until it leaves the sides of the pan. Remove the pan from the heat and pour the mixture out in a thin layer on baking sheets dusted with icing sugar.

Set the oven at 110°C/225°F/gas ¼. Put the baking sheets in the oven to dry overnight, then turn the paste over in order that it may dry on both sides. Then cut the paste into long, narrow strips. These can be formed into knots or other shapes.

MAKES ABOUT 2.75 kg/6 lb

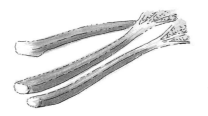

RHUBARB AND LOGANBERRY JAM

900 g/2 lb rhubarb, cut into short lengths
150 ml/¼ pint water
450 g/1 lb loganberries
1.4 kg/3 lb loaf sugar

Stew the rhubarb gently in the water until it is reduced to a thick pulp. Meanwhile pick over the loganberries, add them to the rhubarb and simmer for 5–10 minutes until tender.

Add the sugar and stir over a low heat until the sugar is dissolved. Bring to the boil and boil rapidly until setting point is reached.

Skim. Pour into hot, dry jars and cover.

Note Raspberries may be used instead of loganberries; there is no need to cook them first – just add them with the sugar.

MAKES ABOUT 2.25 kg/5 lb

DAMSON CHEESE

1.1 kg/2½ lb damsons, stalks
removed
loaf sugar

Set the oven at 140°C/275°F/gas 1.

Put the damsons into a large casserole with a little water. Cover closely and cook in the oven for about 2½ hours until perfectly soft. Then push through a fine sieve.

Measure the pulp, and put it into a preserving pan with 350–450 g/ 12 oz–1 lb sugar to every 600 ml/ 1 pint pulp, according to individual taste. Boil until the greater part of the syrup has evaporated and the pulp has become rather stiff, stirring frequently at first and almost continuously towards the end of the process. Turn into hot, dry small jars, and cover closely.

Note The stones may be cracked and the kernels added to the pulp with the sugar.

MAKES ABOUT 2 kg/4½ lb

CRANBERRY AND APPLE JELLY

1.4 kg/3 lb apples
900 g/2 lb cranberries
loaf sugar

Rinse the fruit. Slice the apples, without peeling or coring, and put in a saucepan with the cranberries and sufficient water to cover. Simmer gently until thoroughly mashed. Then strain the pulp through a scalded jelly bag, leaving it to drip undisturbed.

Measure the juice into the cleaned pan. Allow usually 450 g/1 lb sugar to every 600 ml/1 pint juice, but this depends on the pectin content. Bring the juice to the boil. Add the sugar and stir until dissolved, then boil briskly until setting point is reached. Pour into hot, dry jars and cover.

MAKES ABOUT 2 kg/4 ½ lb

LEMON CURD

3 eggs, whisked
75 g/3 oz butter
225 g/8 oz caster sugar
finely grated rind and juice of 2 lemons

Put the eggs in a bowl with the butter, sugar, lemon rind and juice. Place the bowl over a saucepan of boiling water, and stir until the mixture is thick and smooth.

Pour into hot, dry jars and cover.

MAKES ABOUT 350 g/12 oz

ℳARMALADES

Orange marmalade was originally eaten as a sweetmeat or medicine. The Scots were responsible for introducing it to the breakfast table and it is now a standard feature of the British breakfast.

DARK COARSE-CUT MARMALADE

900 g/2 lb Seville oranges
1 lemon
4 litres/7 pints water
2.75 kg/6 lb loaf sugar
15 ml/1 tbsp black treacle

Wash the fruit, cut in half and squeeze the juice. Tie the pips loosely in a muslin bag. Slice the skins into medium-thick shreds. Put the juice, muslin bag, sliced peel and water into a preserving pan and simmer until the peel is tender and the liquid reduced by *at least* one-third (about 1½– 2 hours).

Remove the bag of pips, after squeezing the juice out gently.

Remove the pan from the heat, then add the sugar and treacle, return to the heat and stir over a low heat until the sugar is dissolved. Then boil rapidly until setting point is reached. Pour into hot, dry jars and cover.

MAKES ABOUT 4.5 kg/10 lb

PEACH AND PINEAPPLE MARMALADE

1 large ripe pineapple
3.25 kg/7 lb peaches
3 lemons
2.75 kg/6 lb loaf sugar

Pare and slice the pineapple. Peel and stone the peaches; crack half the stones and remove the kernels. Put the peaches and pineapple into a preserving pan with just a little water to protect the bottom layer, heat slowly to simmering point, and then cook gently for about 30 minutes. Add the sugar gradually, so as not to reduce the temperature below simmering point, the strained juice of the lemons and the kernels, and boil gently for about 20 minutes, skimming when necessary. Pour into hot, dry jars, and cover closely.

MAKES ABOUT 4.5 kg/10 lb

THE ORIGINAL
MARMALADE

Records show that a preserve called 'marmalade', made from the marmelo or quince, was imported into Britain from Portugal before the sixteenth century. Quinces had long been used in physicians' recipes, and were thought to aid digestion. Before the sixteenth century preserves were always referred to as marmalades of damsons or whatever fruit was used.

But by the early 1500s the word was only used to mean a preserve of quinces.

The first recipe for marmalade to be published in English appeared in 1562 and gave instructions for a quince pulp to be boiled with sugar, and flavoured with spices.

muslin bag and put into a preserving pan with the fruit, the peel and all the liquid. Peel and dice the apple and pear and add to the other fruit. Bring to the boil, simmer for 1 ¼ hours or until reduced by one-third. Remove the muslin bag. Add the sugar, stir over a low heat until dissolved. Bring to the boil and boil rapidly until set (about 30 minutes). Cool slightly, then pour into hot, dry jars and cover.

MAKES ABOUT 2.25 kg/5 lb

FIVE-FRUIT MARMALADE

900 g/2 lb fruit: 1 orange,
1 grapefruit, 1 lemon, 1 large apple,
1 pear
1.75 litres/3 pints water
1.4 kg/3 lb loaf sugar

Wash and peel the orange, grapefruit and lemon. Shred the peel finely. Cut this fruit coarsely. Put the pips and coarse tissue in a bowl with 300 ml/½ pint of the water. Put the peel and cut citrus fruit into a bowl with the remaining water. Soak for 24 hours.

Strain the pips and tissue, tie in a

CHUTNEYS AND PICKLES

It is a matter of personal taste as to what sort of chutney should accompany which dishes. Most are excellent with cheese, curries, spiced meat and fish, salads, cold meats and pies.

PLUM CHUTNEY

1.4 kg/3 lb plums, stoned and quartered
2 onions, chopped
2 apples, peeled, cored and chopped
60 ml/4 tbsp ground ginger
60 ml/4 tbsp ground cinnamon
60 ml/4 tbsp allspice
15 ml/1 tbsp salt
about 600 ml/1 pint vinegar
350 g/12 oz loaf sugar

Put the plums, onions, apples, spices and salt and half the vinegar into a preserving pan. Bring to the boil slowly and simmer until the mixture begins to thicken (about 1 hour). Add some of the remaining vinegar gradually until the mixture is thick and smooth, stirring constantly. Add the sugar and if necessary a little more of the vinegar, then boil rapidly until the chutney is the consistency of thick jam. Pour into hot, dry jars and seal immediately.

MAKES ABOUT 1.8 kg/4 lb

RED TOMATO CHUTNEY

900 g/2 lb tomatoes, peeled
1 cooking apple, peeled, cored and
sliced
1 onion, sliced
175 g/6 oz sultanas, chopped
75 g/3 oz dates, chopped
15 ml/1 tbsp mixed whole spice
25 g/1 oz salt
300 ml/½ pint white wine or cider
vinegar
225 g/8 oz soft dark brown sugar

Put the tomatoes, apple, onion, sultanas and dates in a preserving pan. Add the spice, tied in a muslin bag, the salt and 150 ml/¼ pint of the vinegar. Bring to the boil slowly and simmer until the mixture begins to thicken (about 45 minutes). Add the remaining vinegar and the sugar and stir until the sugar is dissolved. Bring to the boil and simmer gently until the mixture is thick. Pour into hot, dry jars and seal immediately.

MAKES ABOUT
1.6 kg/3½ lb

Make a syrup by boiling together 450 ml/¾ pint of the vinegar and the sugar. Put the remaining vinegar into a preserving pan with the mangoes. Bring to the boil and simmer gently for about 10 minutes. Then add the tamarinds, raisins, ginger, cinnamon and nutmeg. Cook very slowly for about 30 minutes, adding the syrup gradually during the last 10 minutes. Boil the mixture until the greater part of the syrup is absorbed, stirring constantly. Pour into hot, dry jars and cover.

MAKES ABOUT
1.6 kg/3½ lb

MANGO CHUTNEY

100 g/4 oz salt
12 ripe mangoes, peeled and thinly sliced
900 ml/1½ pints white wine or cider vinegar
350 g/12 oz loaf sugar
225 g/8 oz tamarinds, stoned
100 g/4 oz seedless raisins
100 g/4 oz green ginger, sliced
1.25 ml/¼ tsp ground cinnamon
1.25 ml/¼ tsp ground nutmeg

Sprinkle the salt over the mangoes and leave for 36 hours, then drain well.

A TASTE OF
THE RAJ

The word chutney comes from the Hindu 'chatni' which was first recorded in 1813 and meant a pulverized mixture of fruits, vegetables, spices and vinegar. These concoctions were served as snacks before a meal or with the main dishes.

The British began to take an interest in Indian food and spices when the first trading posts were established in India in the early seventeenth century. Recipes for chutneys and pickles started appearing in cookery books in the early nineteenth century and Mrs Beeton included instructions in the *Book of Household Management* for making 'Indian Chetney Sauce'. In the later days of the British raj, Indian cooks often taught their memsahibs how to use spice mixtures to make authentic chutneys and Indian dishes.

SUCCESSFUL CHUTNEYS AND PICKLES

If a recipe involves boiling vinegar, an unchipped enamel pan is best since the acid in the vinegar may react badly with brass, copper or iron. For the same reason use only wooden spoons for stirring.

Pickles and chutneys should always be made from fresh, slightly underripe fruit and vegetables.

Vinegar should contain at least 5 per cent acetic acid and only the best quality should be used. Use fresh spices for a full flavour and remember, when tasting chutneys during the cooking process, that the mixture is always spicier when first made. The flavours will mellow with time.

Pot pickles and chutneys in glass or stone jars and be sure that pickles are completely covered with vinegar before sealing the jar.

MUSHROOM KETCHUP

Mushrooms intended for this purpose should be gathered on a dry day, otherwise the ketchup will not keep. Trim the tips of the stalks, but do not wash or peel the mushrooms; simply rub any unclean parts with a little salt. Put the mushrooms in a large jar, sprinkling each layer liberally with salt. Leave for 3 days, stirring them at least three times daily. Then cook them very gently until the juice flows freely. Strain the mushrooms through muslin and drain well, but do not squeeze them.

Replace the liquor in the jar. To every 1.1 litres/2 pints mushroom liquor add 15 g/½ oz allspice, 15 g/½ oz ground ginger, 1.25 ml/¼ tsp pounded mace, and 1.25 ml/¼ tsp cayenne. Stand the jar in a saucepan of boiling water, and cook very gently for 3 hours. Strain two or three times through fine muslin when quite cold. Pour into small screw-topped bottles.

RASPBERRY VINEGAR

1.8 kg/4 lb raspberries
2.25 litres/4 pints white wine vinegar
loaf sugar

Put the raspberries and vinegar into a large jar and stand in a cool place. Stir the mixture two or three times daily for 10 days, then strain off the vinegar. Measure it, adding about 50 g/2 oz sugar to every 600 ml/1 pint. Put in a saucepan, bring to the boil and skim thoroughly. When cold, pour into screw-topped bottles.

MAKES ABOUT 2.25 litres/4 pints

$\mathscr{P}$RESERVED FRUIT

*Candied fruits make a colourful and attractive gift and are
excellent as an after-dinner sweetmeat. Fruits preserved in
alcohol are a treat served as a dessert in winter when fresh
fruits are scarce.*

CRYSTALLIZED FRUITS

A mixture of apricots, greengages
and pineapple is particularly pretty
arranged in a gift box with a clear
lid.

Choose fruit that is not quite
ripe. First blanch the prepared fruit
in boiling water until tender, then
dip into cold water. Boil the fruit in
sugar syrup for a few minutes.
Remove the fruit and place on a
wire rack set over a baking sheet.
Allow to dry in the oven set at
120°C/250°F/gas ½. Then boil the
syrup to the 'large blow' degree
(112°C/233°F). Allow it to cool a

little before dipping the fruit in it until thoroughly coated. Roll the fruit immediately in crushed loaf sugar and leave to dry on a wire rack in the oven.

Apricots – remove the stones by running the point of a small knife into the fruit near the stalk and turning it slightly round the stone which can be gently squeezed out.

Greengages – prick all over with a large darning needle.

Pineapple – cut off the top and stalk and pare off the rind. Then prick to the core in several places with a large darning needle. Put the pineapple in a saucepan, cover with water and bring to the boil. Boil until tender and cut into small wedges.

SUGAR SYRUP

Put 450 g/1 lb loaf sugar and 300 ml/½ pint water in a saucepan, bring to the boil slowly and boil for a few minutes after the sugar is dissolved. Remove from the heat and skim. Return to the heat and boil for another minute or so to reach the 'small thread' degree (101°C/215°F).

CRYSTALLIZED CHESTNUTS

Remove the outer skin and blanch the chestnuts in boiling water until a needle pierces them easily. Then take off the inner skin and rinse in warm water. Drain and put them into a saucepan of sugar syrup. Simmer gently until the syrup becomes thick – the syrup should never be allowed to boil. Remove the chestnuts and drain them in a sieve.

Boil the syrup to the 'small blow' degree (110°C/230°F) and leave until almost cold, then work it against the side of the pan. Using a fork, dip the chestnuts into the syrup, then place on baking sheets and dry in the oven set at 120°C/250°F/gas ½.

PRESENTING
PRESERVES

Cover the tops of jars with brightly coloured fabrics cut into circles large enough to leave about 4 cm/ 1½ inches overhanging the edge of the pot. Hem the edges or cut with pinking shears and fix in place with coloured elastic bands or satin ribbons bearing a pretty gift tag that tones with the fabric.

Cut similar covers from metallic gift-wrap papers and fix in place.

Decorate glass jars with gloss paint – a border around the lower edge, the name of the preserve or a greeting – in colours to tone with the fruit in the jar, or stick silver and gold stars around the outside.

Cut labels of different shapes from colourful paper and attach to the jar or pot. Write the name of the preserve in coloured ink or with a silver or gold spirit pen.

QUEENSLAND HONEY FRUIT COMPOTE

225 g/8 oz dried prunes
225 g/8 oz dried apricots
225 g/8 oz dried figs
225 g/8 oz dried peaches
275 g/10 oz clear honey
600 ml/1 pint water
thinly pared rind of 1 lemon

Soak the dried fruits in water for 8 hours. Drain.

Dissolve the honey in the water and boil, together with the lemon rind, for 5 minutes. Remove the rind.

Pack the fruits into sterilized preserving jars. Cover with the syrup to within 1 cm/½ inch of the top of the jars. Stand the jars on a rack in a deep preserving pan and add warm water to come level with the neck of the jars. Bring to the boil and boil for 3 minutes to expel the air from the jars. Cover with the lids, and screw down to seal. Continue boiling for 25 minutes.

Remove the jars to a wire rack to cool.

MAKES ABOUT 1.1 kg/2 lb

PEARS AND CHERRIES IN WHITE PORT

600 ml/1 pint white port
900 g/2 lb sugar
600 ml/1 pint water
piece of cinnamon stick
450 g/1 lb Morello cherries
1.8 kg/4 lb pears, peeled, cored and halved
a little yellow **or** *orange food colouring*

Put the port, sugar, water and cinnamon stick into a saucepan and bring to the boil. Add the cherries (unstoned) and simmer until the syrup is thick and the cherries almost tender.

Add the pear halves and bring the syrup to the boil once more. Simmer for 2–3 minutes, but do not allow the pears to soften. Stir in the colouring and pour immediately into sterilized jars, until the syrup is about to overflow, and seal.

MAKES ABOUT 2.75 kg/6 lb

$\mathcal{B}$ISCUITS

Freshly baked biscuits make an unusual and very personal gift. Decorative cutters produce shapes to suit Christmas or birthday celebrations or dinner parties. Store the biscuits carefully in an airtight tin to keep them crisp.

GERMAN SPICE BISCUITS

fat for greasing
100 g/4 oz plain flour
50 g/2 oz caster sugar
1.25 ml/¼ tsp mixed spice
75 g/3 oz margarine
flour for rolling out

Grease a baking sheet. Set the oven at 160°C/325°F/gas 3.

Mix the flour, sugar and spice in a bowl. Rub in the margarine until the mixture binds together and forms a pliable dough.

Roll out on a floured board to a thickness of 5 mm/¼ inch and cut into circles with a 6 cm/2½ inch cutter. Place on the prepared baking sheet. Bake for about 20 minutes until very pale gold in colour. Leave to stand for a few minutes, then cool on a wire rack.

MAKES ABOUT 12

BRANDY SNAPS

fat for greasing
50 g/2 oz plain flour
5 ml/1 tsp ground ginger
50 g/2 oz margarine
50 g/2 oz soft dark brown sugar
30 ml/2 tbsp golden syrup
10 ml/2 tsp grated lemon rind
5 ml/1 tsp lemon juice

Grease two or three baking sheets. Also grease the handles of several wooden spoons, standing them upside down in a jar until required. Set the oven at 180°C/350°F/gas 4.

Sift the flour and ginger into a bowl. Melt the margarine in a saucepan. Add the sugar and syrup and warm gently, but do not allow to become hot. Remove from the heat and add the sifted ingredients with the lemon rind and juice. Mix well.

Put small spoonfuls of the mixture on to the prepared baking sheets, spacing them well apart to allow for spreading. Bake for 8–10 minutes.

Remove from the oven and leave to cool for a few seconds until the edges just begin to firm. Lift one of the biscuits with a palette knife and roll loosely around the greased handle of one of the wooden spoons. Allow to cool before removing the spoon handle. Repeat with the remaining biscuits.

MAKES 14 TO 18

CHRISTMAS SQUARES

100 g/4 oz sultanas
100 g/4 oz glacé cherries, chopped
100 g/4 oz cut mixed peel
100 g/4 oz dried figs **or** *dates,*
chopped
grated rind of 1 orange
60 ml/4 tbsp rum, brandy **or** *sherry*
225 g/8 oz plain chocolate
100 g/4 oz butter
100 g/4 oz marzipan, cut into small
pieces
100 g/4 oz almond macaroons or
digestive biscuits, coarsely crushed

Put the sultanas, cherries, peel, figs or dates and orange rind in a bowl and sprinkle the rum, brandy or sherry over them. Mix lightly, cover and leave to stand for at least 2 hours, preferably overnight.

Line a 20 cm/8 inch square tin with rice paper. Break the chocolate into squares and put them in a bowl with the butter. Stand the bowl over a saucepan of hot water and stir the chocolate mixture occasionally until it has completely melted. Remove the bowl from the pan and mix in the soaked fruit with any juices. Add the marzipan and crushed biscuits and mix very lightly, trying not to break up the pieces of marzipan.

Turn the mixture into the prepared tin and chill until set. Cut the set mixture into 16 squares and gently ease them out of the tin. The rice paper base is edible.

MAKES 16

BAKING FOR
CHRISTMAS

Gingerbreads, spiced biscuits, mince pies and fruit loaves have been traditionally cooked for centuries around Britain to offer to visitors between Christmas and Twelfth Night. In Northumberland gingerbread was shaped into men to represent Jesus; in Yorkshire it was eaten with cheese; and in Scotland shortbread was offered on New Year's Day.

The festive foods were served with mulled wine or hot spiced ale to the men who sold holly and ivy from door to door, to carol singers and to friends and neighbours who

called with seasonal messages of good cheer. Gifts of cakes and bread were also added to baskets of food that were delivered to the poorer families of the village on Boxing Day.

Like Christmas puddings and cakes, mincemeat was always made a month before Christmas so that the mixture had time to mature. The whole family was involved in the ritual stirring, each person making a wish as they moved the spoon clockwise through the delicious combination of dried fruits, spices and brandy.

Thoroughly grease three or four baking sheets. Set the oven at 180°C/350°F/gas 4.

Sift the flour, bicarbonate of soda and spices into a bowl. In a mixing bowl, beat the butter until soft, add the sugar and continue to beat until light and fluffy. Beat in the honey and egg yolk, then the milk. Fold in the flour mixture.

Knead the dough lightly on a floured surface, then roll out to a thickness of 3mm/⅛ inch. Cut into stars with a 5cm/2 inch star-shaped biscuit cutter. Using a straw, make a small hole in each star. The hole should be on a point, but not too

CHOCOLATE-TIPPED CINNAMON STARS

fat for greasing
350 g/12 oz plain flour
5 ml/1 tsp bicarbonate of soda
10 ml/2 tsp ground cinnamon
2.5 ml/½ tsp ground ginger
150 g/5 oz butter
100 g/4 oz caster sugar
100 g/4 oz clear honey
1 egg yolk
30 ml/2 tbsp milk
flour for rolling out
150 g/5 oz plain chocolate, broken into squares, to decorate

near the edge. Transfer the biscuits to the prepared baking sheets. Bake for about 8 minutes, until golden brown. Cool for a few minutes on the baking sheets, then transfer to wire racks.

Melt the chocolate with 15 ml/ 1 tbsp water in a saucepan over a low heat. Brush the tips of each star generously with chocolate, then place on a wire rack until the chocolate has set. This process may be speeded up if the biscuits are

chilled in the refrigerator.

When the chocolate is firm, thread a length of ribbon through each biscuit for hanging on a Christmas tree.

MAKES ABOUT 60

KOURABIEDES

450 g/1 lb plain flour
450 g/1 lb unsalted butter
150 g/5 oz icing sugar
1 egg yolk
30 ml/2 tbsp brandy
extra icing sugar for coating

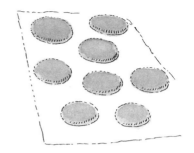

Grease two or three baking sheets.
Set the oven at 180°C/350°F/gas 4.

Sift the flour into a bowl. In a
mixing bowl, cream the butter with
30 ml/2 tbsp of the icing sugar until
light and fluffy. Gradually beat in
the remaining icing sugar and the
egg yolk. Still beating, add the
brandy. Stir in 100 g/4 oz of the
flour and mix well, then fold in the

remaining flour, first using a knife
and then the fingers, to make a soft
dough.

Using a teaspoon, scoop up a
little of the dough. Use a second
teaspoon to transfer the dough to
one of the prepared baking sheets.
Repeat with the remaining dough,
making the heaps about 5 cm/
2 inches apart to allow for
spreading.

Bake for 12–15 minutes or until
pale gold in colour. Cool on the
baking sheets, then sift icing sugar
generously over each biscuit.

MAKES ABOUT 56

OATCAKES

fat for greasing
50 g/2 oz bacon fat **or** *dripping*
100 g/4 oz medium oatmeal
1.25 ml/¼ tsp salt
1.25 ml/¼ tsp bicarbonate of soda
fine oatmeal for rolling out

Grease two baking sheets. Set the oven at 160°C/325°F/gas 3.

Melt the bacon fat or dripping in a large saucepan. Remove from the heat and stir in the dry ingredients, then add enough boiling water to make a stiff dough.

When cool enough to handle, knead the dough thoroughly, then roll out on a surface dusted with fine oatmeal, to a thickness of 5 mm/¼ inch. Cut into wedge-shaped pieces and transfer to the prepared baking sheets. Bake for 20–30 minutes. Cool on a wire rack.

MAKES ABOUT 16

and beat it until it is very soft. Gradually beat in the flour, caraway seeds and salt until the ingredients are thoroughly mixed. Add the beaten eggs and mix well to make a firm dough. Knead the dough briefly on a floured surface, then roll it out thinly and cut out 5 cm/2 inch circles.

Place the crackers on the prepared baking sheets and brush them with a little milk, then bake them for about 12–15 minutes. Transfer the crackers to a wire rack to cool.

MAKES ABOUT 30

CARAWAY CRACKERS

fat for greasing
50 g/2 oz butter
225 g/8 oz plain flour
15 g/½ oz caraway seeds
good pinch of salt
1 egg, beaten
milk to glaze

Grease two baking sheets. Set the oven at 180°C/350°F/gas 4.
Put the butter in a small bowl

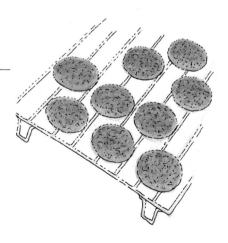

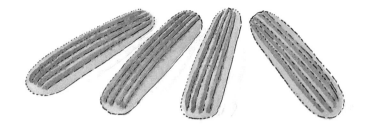

COFFEE TRUFFLE FINGERS

150 ml/¼ pint double cream
15 ml/1 tbsp instant coffee
225 g/8 oz milk chocolate
12–15 sponge fingers
icing sugar

Pour the cream into a small saucepan and add the instant coffee. Heat the mixture gently until the cream boils, then remove the pan from the heat and allow the cream mixture to cool until it is hand-hot.

Break the chocolate into squares and place them in a bowl over a saucepan of hot, not boiling, water. Stir the chocolate occasionally until it has melted, then remove the bowl from the pan.

Pour the cream mixture into the chocolate, stirring all the time, then leave the mixture to cool, stirring it occasionally.

When the mixture begins to thicken, beat it hard with a wooden spoon or use an electric beater to whip it until it is very creamy and light. Chill the whipped mixture until it is firm enough to pipe. It should have formed a thick paste but it should not be allowed to become hard.

Fit a piping bag with a fairly large star nozzle and put the truffle mixture into it. Pipe lines of truffle mixture down the sponge fingers and dust them lightly with a little icing sugar. Chill until firm. To pipe the truffle mixture successfully, keep your hands as cool as possible by placing them under cold running water. If your hands are very warm they will melt the mixture as you hold the piping bag.

MAKES ABOUT 20

$\mathscr{S}$WEETMEATS

Home-made sweets are fun to make, attractive to package and deliciously wicked to eat. Offer as a small gift for Christmas or a child's birthday, or as a contribution to a dinner party.

COCONUT ICE

1.4 kg/3 lb loaf sugar
300 ml/½ pint water
225 g/8 oz desiccated coconut
vanilla essence
carmine colouring

Line a shallow tin with greaseproof paper. Put the sugar and water in a saucepan and boil, without stirring, until the syrup registers 115°C/ 240°F on a sugar thermometer, the 'soft ball' stage. Remove the pan from the heat, add the coconut, and flavour to taste with vanilla essence.

Allow the mixture to cool a little, then pour half into the prepared tin, and stand the pan containing the remainder in hot water, to prevent it setting.

As soon as the portion in the tin is set, add a few drops of carmine food colouring to the mixture in the pan, and pour it over the ice in the tin. When cold, turn out and cut into bars.

MAKES ABOUT
1.6 kg/3½ lb

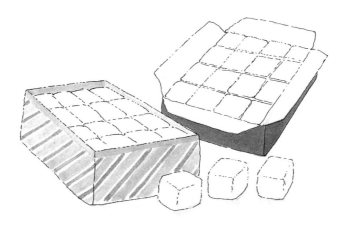

TURKISH DELIGHT

1 orange
1 lemon
450 g/1 lb loaf sugar
150 ml/¼ pint water
25 g/1 oz gelatine
15 ml/1 tbsp rum
50 g/2 oz almonds **or** *pistachios,*
blanched and coarsely chopped
225 g/ 8 oz icing sugar
5–10 ml/1–2 tsp cornflour

Remove the rinds of the orange and lemon in thin fine strips, and put in a saucepan with the loaf sugar, water and the strained juice of the orange and lemon. Bring to the boil, add the gelatine, and simmer until dissolved, stirring constantly. Then strain into a basin and add the rum.

Leave the mixture until on the point of setting, then stir in the almonds or pistachios and pour at once into a wetted tin. When perfectly set turn the jelly out, cut it into 2.5 cm/1 inch squares and dust them lightly in a mixture of icing sugar and cornflour.

MAKES ABOUT 575 g/1¼ lb

THE RIGHT DEGREE

It is easier and safer to use a saccharometer (a sugar thermometer) than to test the syrup with your fingers.

Small Thread (101°C/215°F) – when a short, fine thread is formed when the forefinger is dipped into the solution, touched to the thumb and drawn apart.

Large Thread (103°C/217°F) – when a longer thread is formed.

Small Pearl (105°C/220°F) – when a longer, thicker thread is formed.

Large Pearl (106°C/222°F) – when thumb and finger may be stretched as far as possible without breaking the thread.

Small Blow (110°C/230°F) – when a little of the solution is scooped into a perforated skimming spoon and bubbles are formed when air is blown through the holes in the spoon.

Large Blow or Feathers (112°C/233°F) – when more bubbles are formed and fly off the spoon like feathers.

Small Ball (114°C/237°F) – when a small drop of sugar solution hardens in cold water to form a soft ball.

Large Ball (120°C/247°F) – when a larger ball is formed.

Small or Soft Crack (144°C/290°F) – when the sugar partially sets and sticks to the teeth when bitten.

Large or Hard Crack (150°C/312°F) – when a drop sets hard and brittle in cold water.

BUTTERSCOTCH

oil for greasing
450 g/1 lb loaf sugar
300 ml/½ pint milk
pinch of cream of tartar
225 g/8 oz butter

Put the sugar and milk in a saucepan and stir occasionally over a low heat until the sugar is dissolved. Add the cream of tartar, and the butter a small piece at a time, and boil the mixture until a little, dropped into cold water, forms a moderately hard ball.

Pour into an oiled tin, and as soon as the butterscotch is sufficiently firm, mark off into small oblongs or squares, and when cold, divide the sections. Wrap each piece first in waxed paper, then in foil.

MAKES ABOUT 675 g/1½ lb

TREACLE TOFFEE

butter for greasing
450 g/1 lb soft dark brown sugar
225 g/8 oz black treacle
50 g/2 oz butter
30 ml/2 tbsp water
15 ml/1 tbsp orange juice

Put all the ingredients into a saucepan and allow the sugar to dissolve over a low heat. Boil to the 'small crack' degree (144°C/290°F) and pour into a buttered tin.

Mark into squares when partially set and break when firm. Wrap in waxed paper and store in an airtight tin.

MAKES ABOUT 675 g/1½ lb

SUCCESSFUL SWEETMEATS

By measuring ingredients carefully and by working with the right utensils, amateur sweet-makers should have no difficulty in producing delicious sweetmeats. For the best results the following equipment is needed:

** A large heavy saucepan with a tight-fitting lid.

** A metal hot plate to place over gas burners when a very low steady heat is required.

** A perforated skimming spoon for removing scum.

** A long-handled wooden spatula for stirring.

** A saccharometer that clips to the side of the pan.

** Flat baking sheets or shallow tins in which to set sweets.

** A sharp knife for marking or cutting toffee, butterscotch and fudge.

FUDGE

oil for greasing
450 g/1 lb granulated sugar
150 ml/¼ pint milk
50 g/2 oz butter
2.5 ml/½ tsp vanilla essence

Put the sugar and milk in a saucepan and leave to soak for 1 hour. Add the butter, place over a gentle heat and stir until the sugar is dissolved. Then bring to the boil and boil to the 'small ball' degree (114°C/237°F). Remove from the heat and stir in the vanilla. Cool slightly, then beat until thick. Pour into an oiled tin; cut in squares when cold.
Note Add 30 ml/2 tbsp cocoa or 50 g/2 oz plain chocolate with the butter to make chocolate fudge.

MAKES ABOUT 450 g/1 lb

GIFT-WRAPPED
SWEETS

Line the base of a brightly coloured cardboard box with tissue paper or a colourful paper napkin and arrange the sweets on top. Seal the box and tie up, parcel fashion, with satin ribbon.

Fill a china bowl, box or dish with sweets. Cover with cling film and decorate with a single fresh or silk flower, a sprig of evergreen, a ribbon bow or a decorative label.

Decorate a glass storage jar with a hand-painted design and fill with sweets. Tie a ribbon around the neck.

Fill cellophane packets with sweets, leaving enough space to gather the top into a neat frill. Thread a ribbon or silk thread through a pretty label and tie round.

PEPPERMINT CREAMS

2 large egg whites, stiffly beaten
*1–2 drops oil of peppermint **or** 10 ml/*
2 tsp peppermint essence
450 g/1 lb icing sugar, sifted

Add the stiffly beaten egg whites and the peppermint flavouring to the icing sugar. A very little green colouring may be added if liked. Mix all together thoroughly to a firm dough-like ball and roll out, well sifted with icing sugar, to a thickness of about 3–5 mm/⅛–¼ inch. Cut out with a small round sweet cutter and leave on a wire rack to dry out for 12 hours. Pack into an air-tight container.

The creams may be coated with melted chocolate if desired. For this, dissolve some broken chocolate in a bowl over hot water and dip the creams into the chocolate, holding them on a fine skewer or a sweet-dipping fork. Allow to set on greaseproof paper.

MAKES ABOUT 450 g/1 lb

$\mathscr{F}$ESTIVE FARE

*Mincemeat and brandy butter have been popular in
Britain as part of Christmas celebrations for hundreds of
years. Mincemeat should be made well in advance of the
festivities so that flavours have time to mature.*

MINCEMEAT

*575 g/1¼ lb cooking apples, peeled
and cored (prepared weight)
450 g/1 lb currants
450 g/1 lb seedless raisins
225 g/8 oz sultanas
100 g/4 oz candied peel
450 g/1 lb beef suet
450 g/1 lb soft dark brown sugar
grated rind and juice of 2 lemons
5 ml/1 tsp ground nutmeg
1.25 ml/¼ tsp ground cloves
1.25 ml/¼ tsp ground cinnamon
2.5 ml/½ tsp salt
75 ml/3 fl oz brandy*

Put the apples, dried fruit, candied
peel and suet through a mincer or
food processor. Add the other
ingredients and mix well. Fill into
jars and cover.

MAKES ABOUT 2.75 kg/6 lb

BRANDY BUTTER

*75 g/3 oz butter
175 g/6 oz icing sugar, sifted
5–15 ml/1 tsp–1 tbsp brandy*

Cream the butter until soft. Add
the icing sugar and cream it with
the butter until white and light in
texture. Work the brandy carefully
into the mixture. Store in an
airtight jar.
Note A stiffly whisked egg white
may be folded into the mixture
before serving with Christmas or
other steamed puddings.

MAKES ABOUT 250 g/9 oz

$\mathscr{D}$RINKS

A particularly unusual gift at Christmas is a bottle of home-made liqueur, and these two recipes are easy to prepare. Bottled in September, they will be at their peak in December, ready for seasonal celebrations.

CHERRY BRANDY

2.25 kg/5 lb ripe Morello cherries
450 g/1 lb soft dark brown sugar
60 apricot, peach or plum kernels
25 g/1 oz bitter almond, shredded
3.5 cm/1¼ inch piece of cinnamon stick
about 1.75 litres/3 pints brandy

Trim the cherry stalks, leaving about 1 cm/½ inch on each one.

Prick the fruit well with a coarse darning needle.

Half-fill some wide-necked preserving jars with the prepared fruit. Divide the sugar, kernels, almond and cinnamon between the jars. Fill up the jars with brandy and attach the lids securely. Keep for at least three months before using, shaking the jars occasionally.

Strain through fine muslin into screw-topped bottles.

Note The cherries may be added to trifles.

MAKES ABOUT
1.75 litres/3 pints

BLACKCURRANT LIQUEUR

450 g/1 lb blackcurrants, hulled
350 g/12 oz soft dark brown sugar
900 ml/1½ pints gin

Put the fruit into a wide-necked bottle, add the sugar and pour in the gin. Let it stand for 2 months, then strain through muslin until it is quite clear. Pour into bottles and seal.

Note The liqueur should be stored in a cool, dry place.

MAKES ABOUT
900 ml/1½ pints

◆◆

A LOAF OF SUGAR

When sugar first arrived in Britain with other spices from the Orient in the thirteenth century, it was shaped into flat blocks called sugar cakes. These had to be crushed before the sugar could be used. A process for refining and crystallizing sugar into conical loaves was invented in Venice in the late fifteenth century and this method continued until the late 1800s. The loaves weighed anything between 2.25 kg/5 lb and 16 kg/ 35 lb and were broken into convenient pieces with special choppers and strong iron nippers. Until a high tax was reduced in 1874, sugar was very expensive and poor people had to use low quality, coarse sugar that did not make very good jam.

$\mathcal{I}$NDEX